• JENNY ACKLAND •

At Home with Reading

• Oxford University Press •

How to help your child

- Choose a quiet time to sit together, when your child is not tired or distracted.

- Work in short periods of activity, and stop as soon as your child loses concentration.

- Talk through the activities with your child, and ask for his or her reasons for choices, especially with the *What happens next* sequences.

- Give plenty of praise and encouragement.

- Remember that the workbook should be fun for your child, as well as being educationally worthwhile.

About Reading

The process of learning to read involves all of the following skills:

- – visual perception of individual letter shapes
- – association of letters with sounds
- – anticipation of common sequences of letters and words
- – recognition of shapes of individual words
- – prediction of meaning
- – observation of print in the world around us

Further notes on the individual sections are provided on page 48.

• CONTENTS •

Find the same 4–7

What comes next? 8–11

Letter shapes 12–21

Word recognition 22–27

What happens next? 28–31

Mix and match 32–39

Reading for meaning 40–43

Words around you 44–47

Notes for parents 48

Join up the same

Join up the same

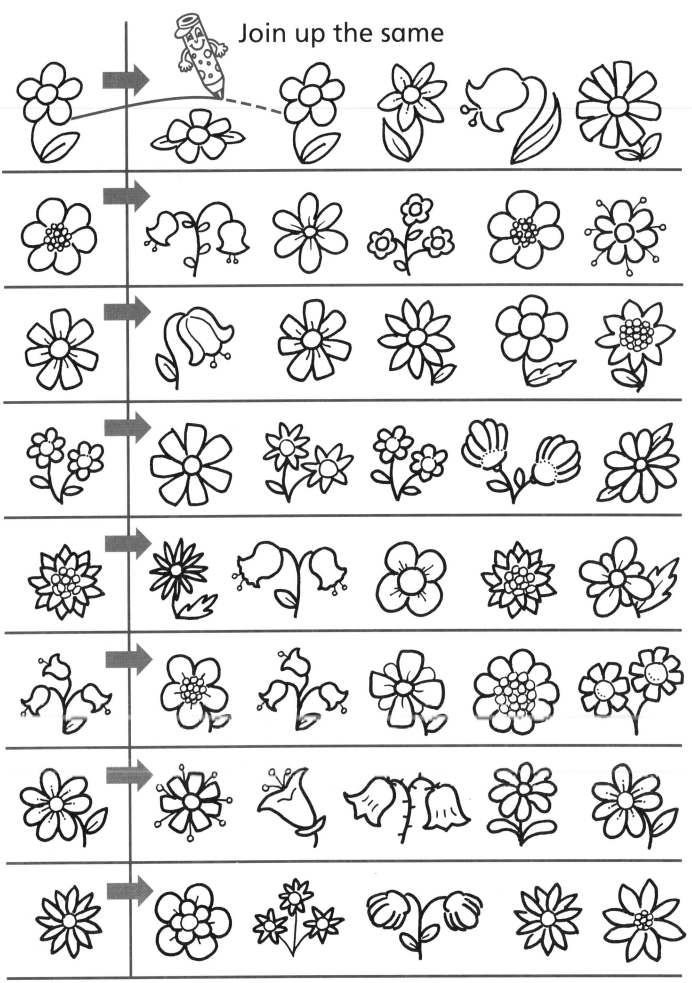

Join up the same

6

Matching pairs

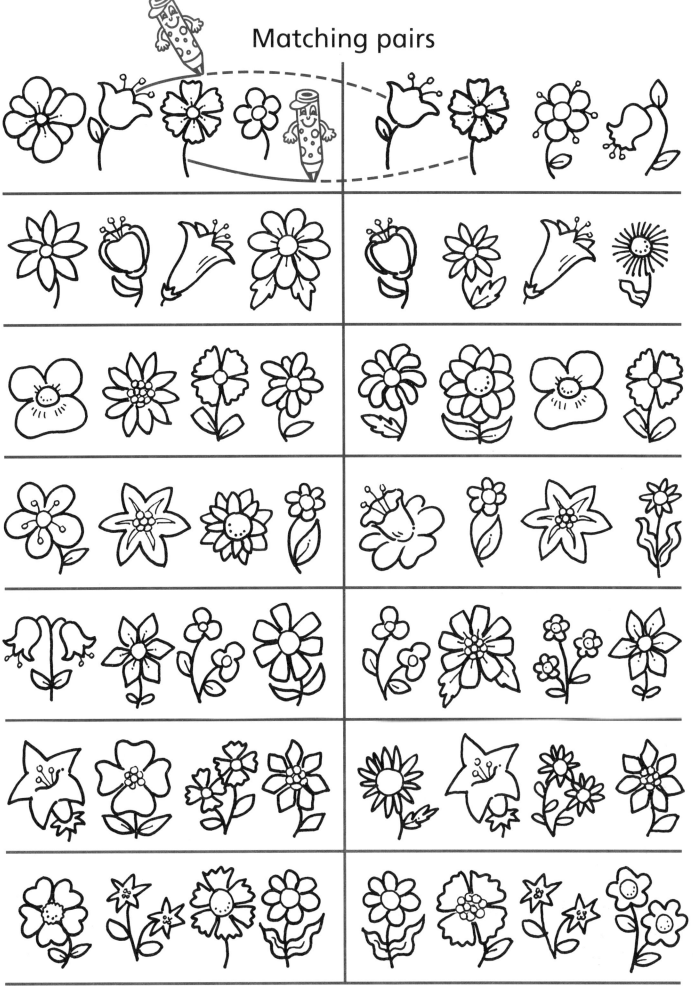

What comes next?

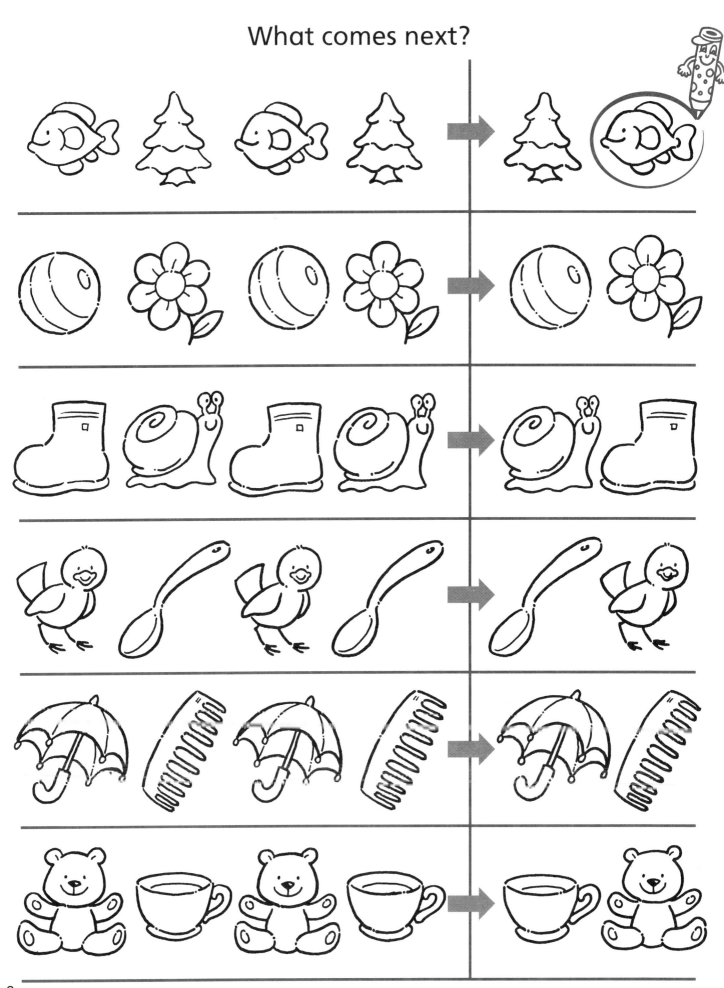

What comes next?

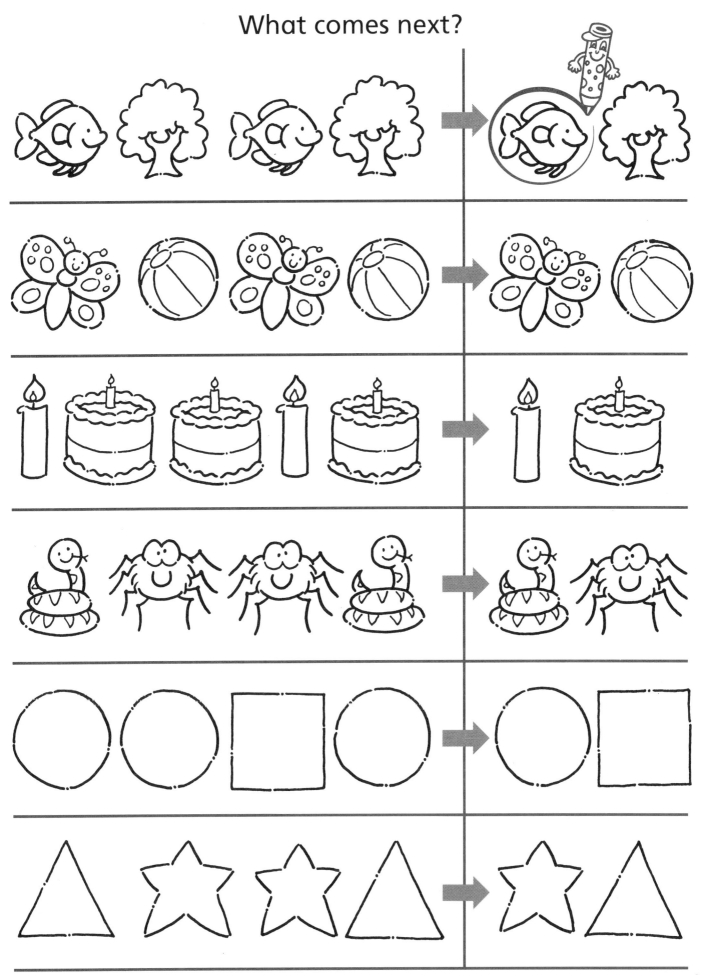

What comes next?

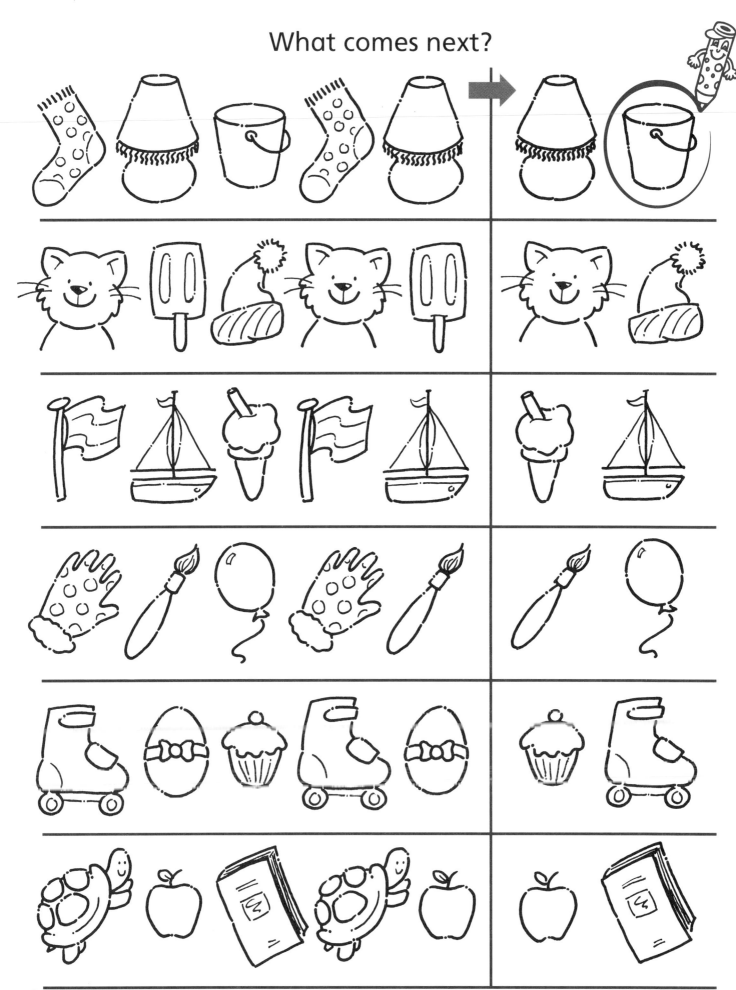

What comes next?

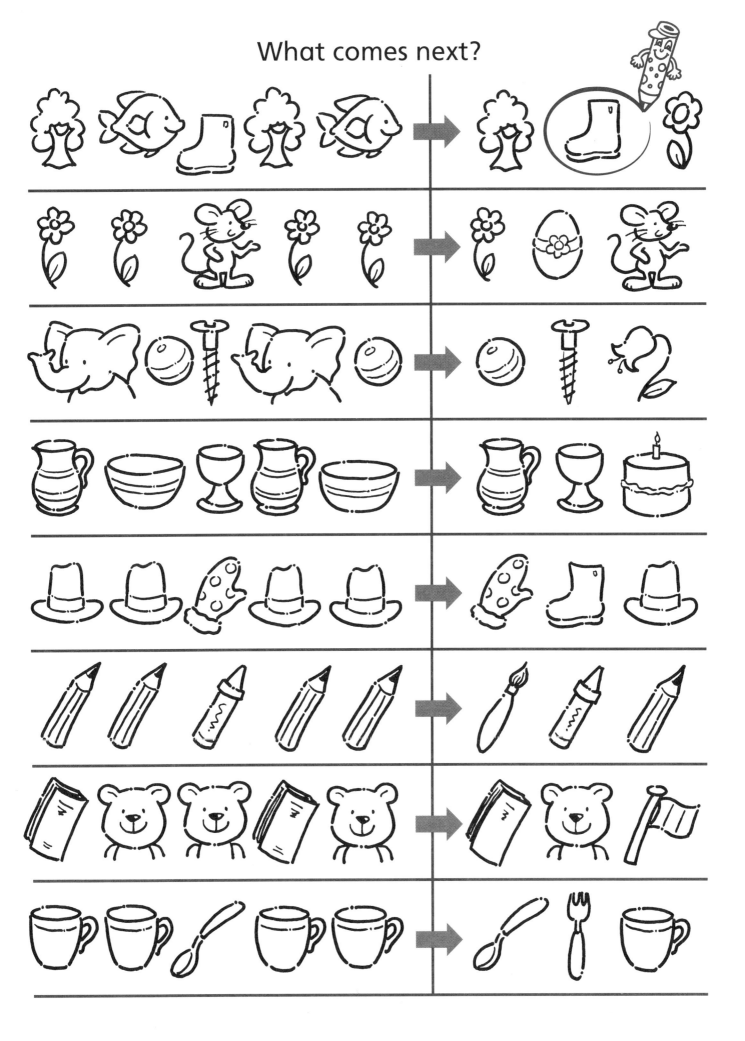

Odd one out

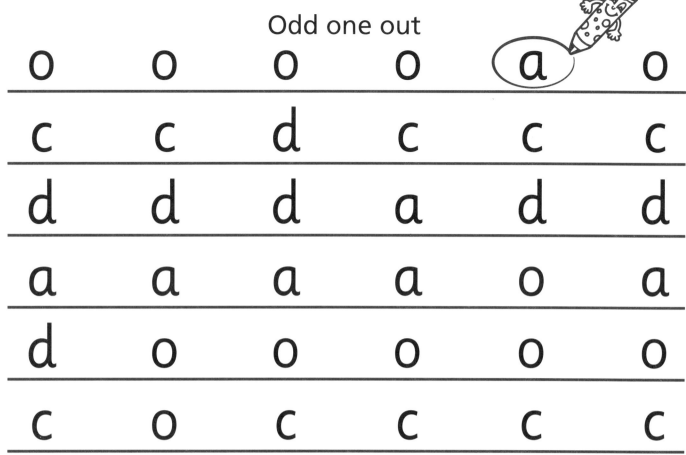

o	o	o	o	a	o
c	c	d	c	c	c
d	d	d	a	d	d
a	a	a	a	o	a
d	o	o	o	o	o
c	o	c	c	c	c

Join up the same

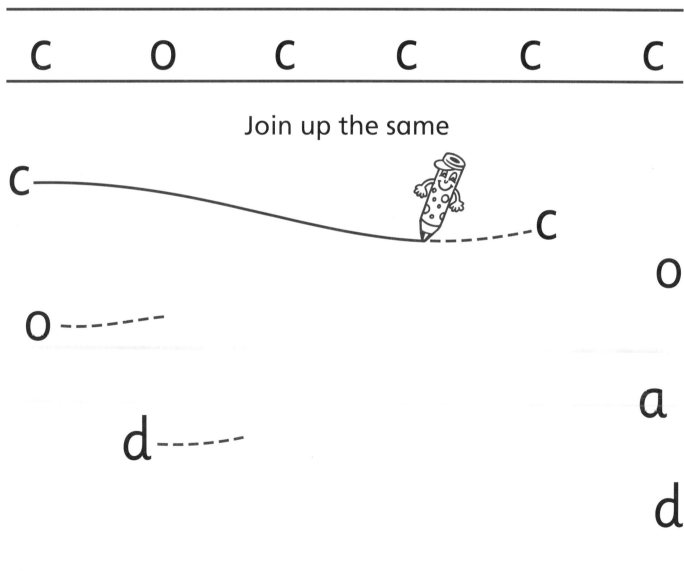

c   c

               o

o

               a

d

               d

a

c o

13

Circle in colour

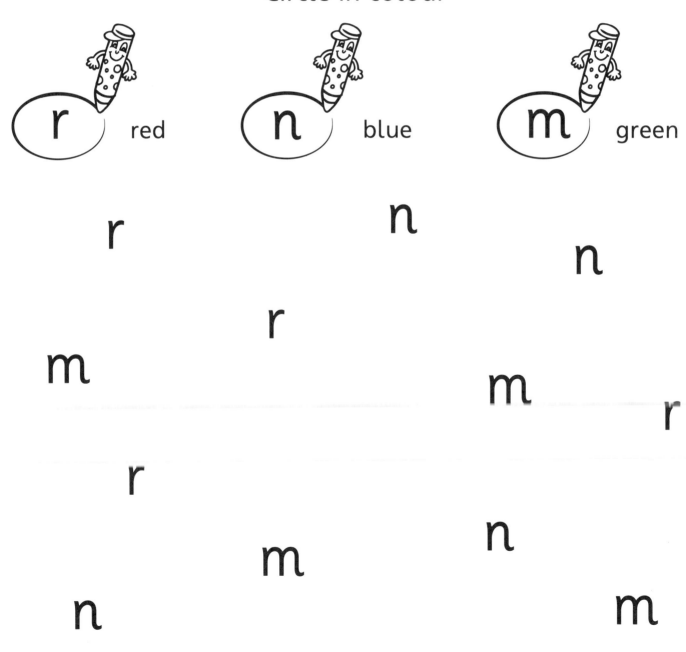

r

n

m

c

d

15

Join up the same

r n m c o a d

Colour the **m**onkeys red.

Colour the **a**pples green.

Colour the **c**ats black.

Colour the **o**ranges orange.

Colour the **n**uts yellow.

Colour the **d**ots blue.

Colour the **r**abbits pink.

Odd one out

r	r	r	r	(h)	r
s	c	c	c	c	c
m	m	n	m	m	m
h	h	h	r	h	h
l	l	l	l	t	l
t	t	h	t	t	t

Join up the same

h   h

s   s

m   m

         n

n

t   t

      l   l

Circle the same letter

c →	t	s	(c)	a	d	n
m →	h	o	d	r	a	m
t →	s	n	n	t	c	r
s →	t	o	r	m	s	d
o →	a	o	t	r	h	l
l →	l	s	m	o	a	n
n →	r	t	a	s	n	d
h →	l	h	o	a	s	t
r →	t	a	r	d	h	s
d →	m	o	t	s	d	h

Join up the same

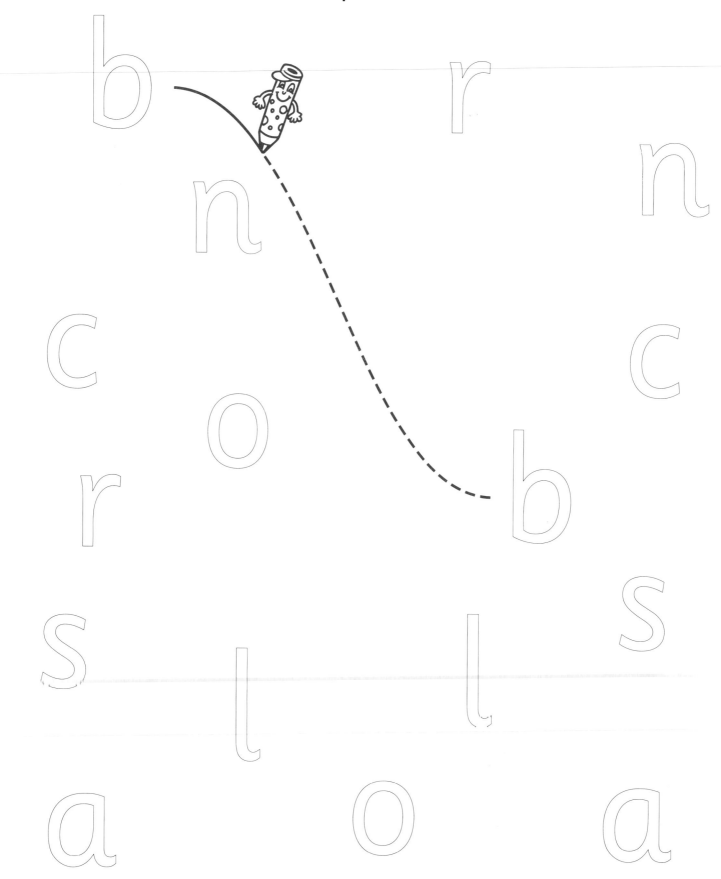

Colour the pairs the same colour

Join up the same

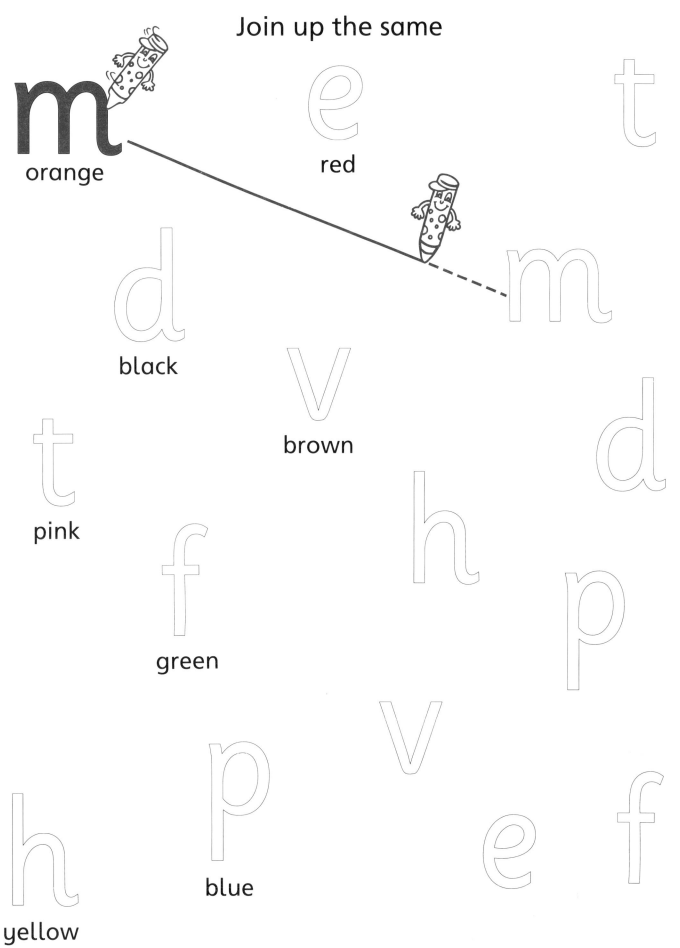

m
orange

e
red

t

m

d
black

v
brown

d

t
pink

h

p

f
green

h
yellow

p
blue

v

e

f

Colour the pairs the same colour

Odd one out

wet	wet	wet	(let)	wet	wet
cat	rat	cat	cat	cat	cat
the	the	she	the	the	the
pig	pig	dig	pig	pig	pig
fun	fun	fun	fun	run	fun
dog	dog	dog	doll	dog	dog
see	see	see	see	bee	see
car	far	car	car	car	car
hat	hat	hat	fat	hat	hat
jam	jam	jam	ham	jam	jam

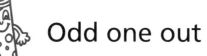

Odd one out

it	it	(on)	it	it	it
the	my	the	the	the	the
for	for	for	school	for	for
cat	off	cat	cat	cat	cat
and	fish	and	and	and	and
my	my	my	dog	my	my
school	see	school	school	school	school
on	on	on	friend	on	on
fish	play	fish	fish	fish	fish
and	friend	friend	friend	friend	friend

Join up the same

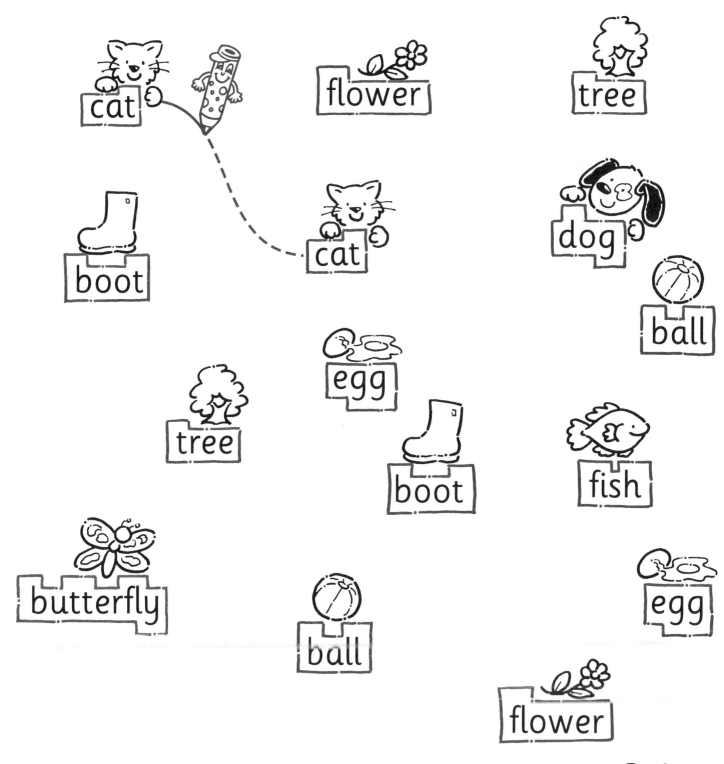

cat

flower

tree

boot

cat

dog

ball

tree

egg

boot

fish

butterfly

ball

egg

flower

fish

dog

butterfly

Find one the same

monkey	me	(monkey)	my	man
apple	and	at	apple	as
orange	off	octopus	on	orange
rabbit	rabbit	run	ring	rat
nuts	net	not	nuts	no
car	caterpillar	cat	car	clock
caterpillar	cup	cake	cut	caterpillar
ring	rose	rag	ring	rod
nail	nanny	nail	nest	nose
donkey	dish	dinner	door	donkey

Find two the same

fish	for	fun	(fish)	fat	(fish)
house	house	hen	hat	house	his
dog	door	dog	dig	dog	dinner
boy	boy	bat	bun	bed	boy
tree	tap	tree	ten	top	tree
egg	end	elf	egg	elephant	egg
book	bit	bag	beg	book	book
jug	jam	jug	jack	jug	jump
kite	kangaroo	kite	kitten	kiss	kite
lamp	lamp	ladder	log	lamp	look

Find two the same

monkey	mum	(monkey)	me	mouse	(monkey)
pig	pig	peg	parrot	pig	pat
rabbit	ring	rabbit	rat	run	rabbit
snail	snail	sock	six	some	snail
apple	ant	apple	apple	an	axe
teddy	ten	teddy	tin	to	teddy
girl	go	get	girl	give	girl
cake	cake	come	cake	cat	cup
bed	bike	bed	ball	balloon	bed
window	water	went	we	window	window

What happens next?

What happens next?

What happens next?

Mark Yes or No

Yes   No

Yes   No

Yes   No

Yes   No

Yes   No

Yes   No

Mark Yes or No

Yes   No

Yes   No

Yes   No

Yes   No

Yes   No

Yes   No

I like ✓   I don't like ✗

baked beans

lemons

pears

bananas

sausages

cheese

sprouts

fish fingers

egg

curry

peas

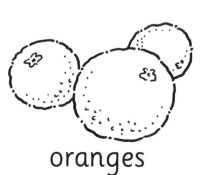

oranges

tomatoes

34

I can ✓   I can't ✗

run

fly

jump

dive

swing

hop

skate

dig

sit

Join up the same

Join up the pets

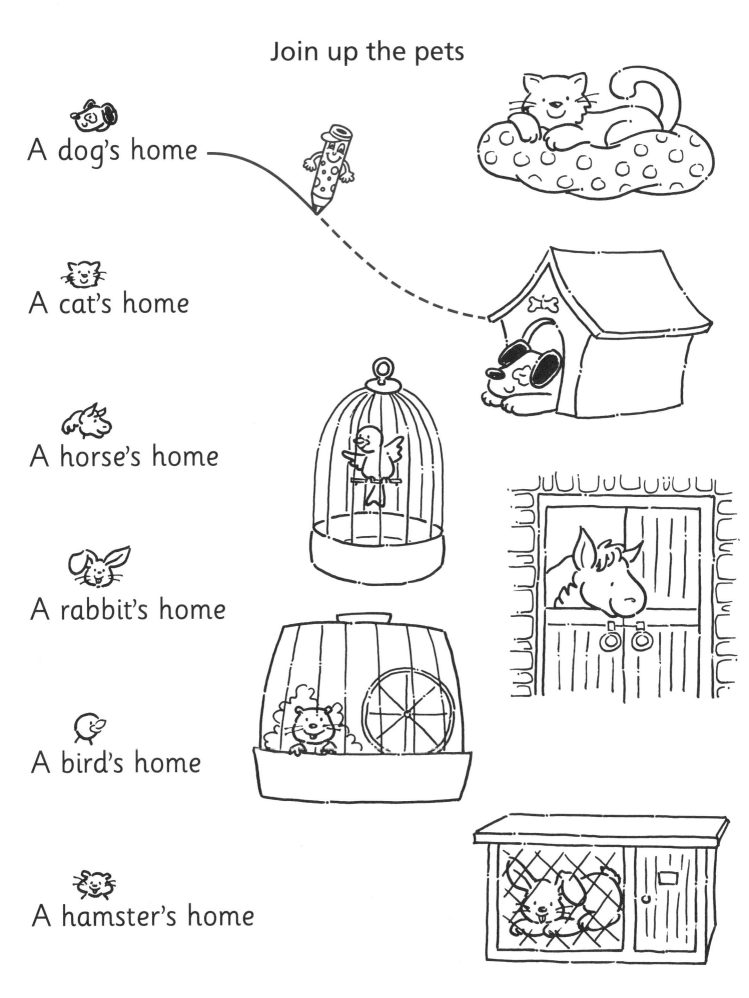

A dog's home

A cat's home

A horse's home

A rabbit's home

A bird's home

A hamster's home

in   on   under

in

on

under

in

on

under

in

on

under

38

in front of   behind

in front of

behind

in front of

behind

in front of

behind

in front of

behind

in front of

behind

in front of

behind

I can see

cat

I can see a   hat

I can see a   dog
car

I can see a   man
dog

I can see a   monkey
cat

I can see a   hat
rabbit

I can see a   apple
hat

I can see an   orange
cake

I can see a   teddy
bed

I can see a   house
man

I can see a   lamp
candle

I can see

I can see a		cake bed
I can see a		nest boot
I can see a		snake rat
I can see a		hat candle
I can see a		lamp bed
I can see a		ladder dog
I can see a		sock door
I can see an		mat apple
I can see a		house monkey
I can see a		rat horse

Jumps over

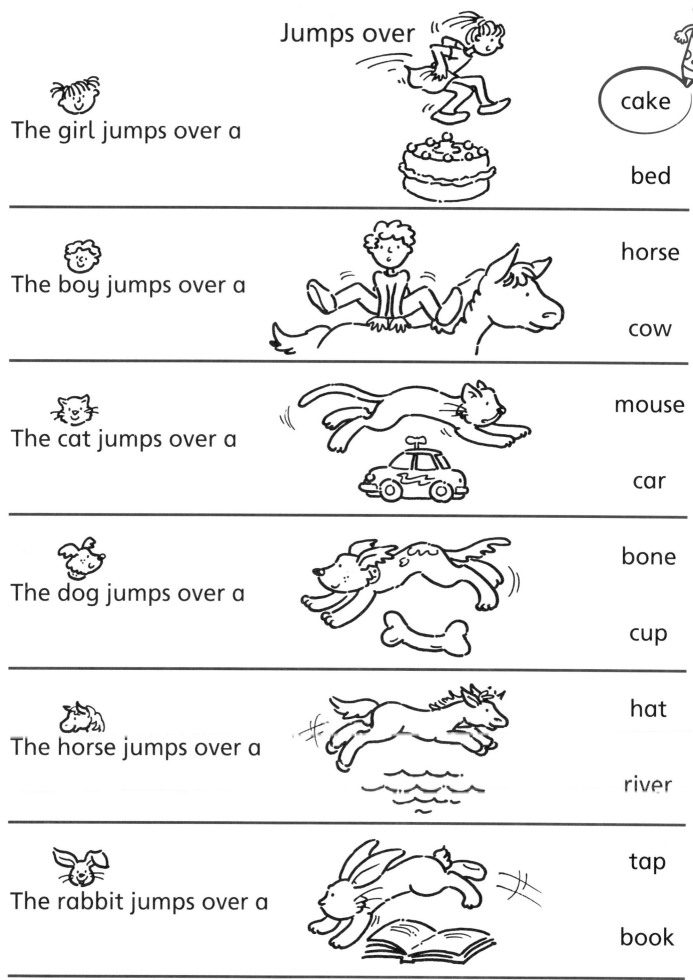

The girl jumps over a

cake

bed

The boy jumps over a

horse

cow

The cat jumps over a

mouse

car

The dog jumps over a

bone

cup

The horse jumps over a

hat

river

The rabbit jumps over a

tap

book

swimming   jumping   running

The dog is swimming.

The cat is jumping.

The boy is running.

The dog is running.

The girl is jumping.

43

Can you read these signs?

Exit

Way in

detergents

biscuits/cakes

tinned food

tea/coffee

salads

frozen fish

45

Can you read these signs?

Notes for parents

Find the same pp. 4–7   This section is about visual discrimination, or helping your child to look closely at pictorial shapes and patterns. This is good preparation for distinguishing between shapes of actual letters. After matching the shapes, the child can colour them in matching colours, to help hand–eye coordination.

What comes next? pp. 8–11   This section practises left-to-right eye movements, in preparation for the motion of reading. It also helps the child anticipate patterns and sequences of shapes, which is a key skill in reading. You may want to cover the rest of the page while the child is reading one line, to help concentration.

Letter shapes pp. 12–21   These letters are deliberately not introduced in alphabetical order: in both handwriting and reading it is easier to introduce letters in 'letter families', i.e. those of similar shape. We therefore start with o, c, a, d; then r, n, m; then l, t and s, h. With each letter you should help your child trace the shape with their finger, then practise the sound; this should be pronounced as a short 'der', not as the name of the letter, 'dee'. You can then progress to linking this initial sound with words beginning with that sound, i.e. duck, donkey, etc, and play I-spy around the home.

We also introduce the colour words at this stage, for you to read out for the child.

Word recognition pp. 22–27   In this section, the visual shape of the word is linked to the object, for visual association. Children often find longer words easier to associate in this way than the short words like 'in' and 'on'. You should help the child sound out the first letter or the whole word each time, then look for words of the same shape. In this way the child will build up a visual memory of common words.

What happens next? pp. 28–31   This section is again about left–right eye movement, and prediction of sequences of action. This kind of logic is very close to the prediction one exercises in reading sequences of meaning. Do talk through these sequences with your child, so that they can explain their choices.

Mix and match pp. 32–39   These are more exercises in logic, to develop children's skills of association between visual images, words, and meaning.

Reading for meaning pp. 40–43   We have now progressed to reading whole sentences, which the child completes by word recognition.

Words around you pp. 44–47   Finally, here are some examples of the opportunities for reading which surround us in everyday life: street signs, labels, notices, all of which provide reading practice for your child at home and in the world around you.

Oxford University Press, Walton Street, Oxford OX2 6DP
Oxford New York
Athens Auckland Bangkok Bombay
Calcutta Cape Town Dar es Salaam Delhi
Florence Hong Kong Istanbul Karachi
Kuala Lumpur Madras Madrid Melbourne
Mexico City Nairobi Paris Singapore
Taipei Tokyo Toronto

and associated companies in Berlin Ibadan

Oxford is a trade mark of Oxford University Press

© Jenny Ackland 1993
First published 1993
Reprinted 1993, 1994 (twice), 1995

ISBN 0 19 838115 8

Designed by Oxprint Ltd, Oxford
Illustrations by Helen Prole
Printed in Hong Kong